RAND NATIONAL SECURITY RESEARCH DIVISION

T0097396

# Countering China's Efforts to Isolate Taiwan Diplomatically in Latin America and the Caribbean

## The Role of Development Assistance and Disaster Relief

Scott W. Harold, Lyle J. Morris, Logan Ma

Sponsored by the Taipei Economic and Cultural Relations Office

For more information on this publication, visit www.rand.org/t/RR2885

**Library of Congress Cataloging-in-Publication Data** is available for this publication.
ISBN: 978-1-9774-0240-0

Published by the RAND Corporation, Santa Monica, Calif.
© Copyright 2019 RAND Corporation
**RAND**® is a registered trademark.

**Support RAND**
Make a tax-deductible charitable contribution at
www.rand.org/giving/contribute

www.rand.org

## Preface

This report describes Taiwan's development assistance and disaster relief programs in Latin America and the Caribbean, exploring how such programs are viewed locally as well as by the United States. In turn, the authors of this report aim to identify areas where Taipei might make further improvements in its giving to encourage countries to continue extending Taiwan diplomatic recognition instead of switching ties to the People's Republic of China, which seeks to poach Taipei's diplomatic partnerships as a strategy to isolate and weaken the island. The report explores Taiwan's giving in two specific cases—Honduras and Haiti—and draws insights from these instances as well as from interviews with U.S. officials and subject-matter experts who shed light on the key factors that shape recognition decisions and what might make diplomatic ties more resilient.

This research was sponsored by the Taipei Economic and Cultural Relations Office (TECRO) and conducted within the International Security and Defense Policy Center of the RAND National Security Research Division (NSRD). NSRD conducts research and analysis for the Office of the Secretary of Defense, the Joint Staff, the Unified Combatant Commands, the defense agencies, the Navy, the Marine Corps, the U.S. Coast Guard, the U.S. Intelligence Community, allied foreign governments, and foundations.

For more information on the RAND International Security and Defense Policy Center, see www.rand.org/nsrd/ndri/centers/isdp or contact the Center director (contact information is provided on the webpage).

# Contents

# Table

# Summary

The Republic of China (ROC, also known as Taiwan)—a liberal democratic republic under threat from the People's Republic of China (PRC, China)—faces a growing challenge as the number of countries that extend it formal diplomatic recognition continues to shrink. In the past, Taiwan spent substantially to compete with China for global diplomatic recognition. Today, however, China's deeper pockets means that Taipei has to spend smarter and give more strategically if it wants to continue to leverage development assistance as an incentive for countries to refrain from swapping recognition to Beijing in exchange for economic rewards.

How can Taiwan optimize its development assistance to Latin America and the Caribbean (regions with the largest number of Taipei's remaining diplomatic partners, and hence a valuable focus for study) to ensure that it gets the maximum diplomatic value out of its generosity? What aid programs does Taiwan currently undertake in the region, and what does it get from their efforts? How does Taiwan's assistance fit with U.S. policy goals and giving in the region? Are there areas where adjustments could be made that would produce synergies between Taiwan and U.S. efforts while also reducing the temptation on the part of regional governments to de-recognize Taipei and switch ties to Beijing?

Through official documents, interviews with key government and international development officials, and case studies of Taiwan's aid to Haiti and Honduras, this study explores these questions and finds that, on the whole, Taiwan's assistance to the governments of Latin America and the Caribbean is well-received, improving desired outcomes such as enhancing local livelihoods and contributing to greater resilience and more rapid disaster recovery and relief. Taiwan's giving is also largely consonant with and additive to U.S. policy goals in the region, and U.S. officials voice strong appreciation of Taipei's programs and actively seek to discourage regional countries from de-recognizing the Republic of China in favor of the PRC. Taiwan's aid programs are also critical for incentivizing countries to continue to stick by Taipei, but official assistance is just one part of a broader and more complicated picture when it comes to countries' decisions on diplomatic recognition. Other important factors include trade and investment, history, and the idiosyncratic policy preferences of leadership in the aid-receiving countries.

A review of Taipei's aid efforts, together with interviews of U.S. experts and officials, reveals a few areas where some improvements could be made that might enhance the prospects that Taiwan can hold onto its official diplomatic ties. These include continued substantial levels of funding and high-level government attention; greater efforts to leverage Taiwan's comparative advantage as an aid partner whose approach to development helps empower the recipient nation; and other steps. At the same time, it is worth bearing in mind that the PRC appears likely to continue to be willing to expend substantial resources to poach Taiwan's diplomatic partnerships, and even generous giving by Taiwan focused on empowering recipient nations and communities as true partners can be trumped by Beijing's deeper pockets and/ or the idiosyncratic calculations of aid recipients and diplomatic partners. For these reasons, a measure of caution and a fallback plan for dealing with the consequences of loss of recognition by countries are warranted. It also may be prudent to mount a broader effort to reposition Taiwan's diplomatic strategy and place in the world—however, such an effort goes beyond the scope of this study, would likely require major research and red-teaming, and would need to be closely guarded lest China seek to block its implementation.

# Acknowledgments

Several people were instrumental in helping to make this report possible. The authors wish to thank the staff at the Taipei Economic and Cultural Relations Office, especially Johnson Chiang, Jared Lin, Daniel Chen, Hanpin Huang, and Mandy Tsai. Katie Taylor, Liza Mantilla, and Aaron van Alstine at the Pan American Development Foundation provided helpful advice and guidance at the outset of the project when the team was conceptualizing the framework of analysis and choosing the cases we ultimately studied. Numerous U.S. government officials, who were promised anonymity to enable them to speak freely, were exceedingly gracious with their time, insights, experiences, and advice and helped us to both understand the issues and the possible policy options available to Taiwan. Several subject-matter experts also contributed valuable assessments and recommendations to the study at various points in time, including our colleagues Michael Chase, Patrick Cronin, Jessica Drun, Chip Gregson, Russell Hsiao, Scott Kastner, and Gerrit van der Wees. Others offered comments at public and closed-door sessions that we found extremely helpful, including Janice Chen, Evan Ellis, Daniel Erickson, and Richard Fisher, Jr. An internal review by Derek Grossman and an external review by Bonnie Glaser also helped us further refine and improve our analytic insights. Of course, any remaining errors or omissions are solely the fault of the authors.

# Abbreviations

| | |
|---|---|
| AIT | American Institute in Taiwan |
| CABEI | Central American Bank for Economic Integration |
| GCTF | Global Cooperation and Training Framework |
| ICDF | International Cooperation and Development Fund |
| IT | information technology |
| LAC | Latin America and the Caribbean |
| MOFA | Ministry of Foreign Affairs |
| NGO | nongovernmental organization |
| OAS | Organization of American States |
| PADF | Pan American Development Foundation |
| PRC | People's Republic of China |
| ROC | Republic of China |
| SME | small and medium enterprises |
| USAID | United States Agency for International Development |
| US | United States dollar (written as "US$") |
| WHO | World Health Organization |

# CHAPTER ONE

# Introduction

The Republic of China (ROC, also known as Taiwan) was founded upon the collapse of the Manchu Great Qing Empire in 1912. It has continued to exist since then, but today, it confronts an existential challenge to its survival as an independent, liberal democratic republic situated on the islands of Taiwan, Penghu, Kinmen, and Matsu from the People's Republic of China (PRC, also referred to as China or mainland China; capital: Beijing). Between the founding of the PRC in 1949 and 2018, the ROC has seen a continued dwindling of its diplomatic recognition; today, Taiwan is recognized by just 17 other nations.[1]

Following a period of intense "dollar" or "checkbook" diplomacy during the 1990s and 2000s when Taipei attempted to hold on to (and even, in some cases, buy back) diplomatic recognition from foreign partners, Taiwan shifted away from a strategy of attempting to match Beijing's deep pockets after nine countries abandoned Taipei for Beijing between 2000 and 2008.[2] From 2008 to 2016, Beijing agreed to a diplomatic truce with Taipei, pausing in its efforts to pry away Taiwan's remaining diplomatic partners and choosing instead to attempt to negotiate terms of economic and potentially political integration with the Ma Ying-jeou administration. However, following the inauguration of Democratic Progressive Party leader Tsai Ing-wen as president in May 2016, China has resumed its campaign to undermine Taiwan's diplomatic recognition, employing astronomical amounts of money to persuade Taipei's remaining partners to switch diplomatic ties to Beijing (Chung, 2018). Since the resumption of China's efforts to sideline Taiwan in 2016, six of the ROC's diplomatic partners, including

---

[1] Taiwan's Ministry of Foreign Affairs regards diplomatic recognition with such importance that its website refers to the 17 countries that recognize the ROC as the nation's "diplomatic allies" (Ministry of Foreign Affairs, Republic of China [Taiwan], 2019).

[2] Further complicating matters, such efforts sometimes required highly flexible and often-secret donation practices, the legalities of which were ambiguous at best and became politically contentious domestically when the Ma Ying-jeou administration charged former Chen Shui-bian administration officials with embezzling funds designed to win diplomatic recognition. While Taiwan claims to have reformed its assistance and done away with bribes and payoffs—which carry the risk of exposure that could cast Taiwan in a negative light—many foreign analysts continue to suspect Taiwan's aid programs of having both above-board and under-the-table aspects (Council on Hemispheric Affairs, 2008; Erikson and Chen, 2007). For more on Taiwan's competition with China for diplomatic recognition in Latin American countries in the 1990s and 2000s not specifically examined in this study, see Alexander, 2014.

Burkina Faso, the Dominican Republic, the Gambia,[3] Sao Tome and Principe, Panama, and El Salvador, have switched recognition from Taipei to Beijing (Ndiaga and Yu, 2018).[4]

In light of the diplomatic pressure China has brought to bear on Taiwan, an increasingly pressing policy issue for Taipei is preventing the ROC's remaining diplomatic partners from abandoning it. What policies might dissuade countries from de-recognizing Taiwan? One option is to leverage the country's development assistance programs to encourage countries to continue to extend diplomatic recognition to the ROC. How much can such programs do to incentivize countries not to break diplomatic relations with Taipei? Which areas of strength can Taiwan draw on in striving to protect its "international living space" (國際生存空間), or its ability to participate in formal international society, either through bilateral relations or multilateral organizations? Are there areas where, by achieving synergies in development assistance with the policies and aid programs of the United States, Taiwan might make it costlier and less attractive for countries to switch recognition to Beijing?

## Study Approach

This study explores the answers to these questions using insights derived from two case studies of Taiwan's aid and assistance programs in Latin America and the Caribbean (LAC). The LAC region is home to nine of the ROC's diplomatic partners (if Paraguay in South America is included), meaning more than half of Taiwan's remaining official diplomatic counterparts reside in the region. Specifically, this study examines Taiwan's development assistance to Honduras and its resiliency, recovery, and disaster relief aid to Haiti. The cases of Honduras and Haiti were chosen after consultation with international development specialists from the Pan American Development Foundation (PADF), an international nongovernmental organization (NGO) that works closely with Taiwan in executing development assistance programs across the region.[5] Because budgetary and time constraints did not permit travel to the region to conduct on-site data collection, some of our conclusions are necessarily tentative due to data limitations; these considerations also factored in our choice of country cases, with Honduras and Haiti being among the countries with the most data publicly available.[6] While

---

[3]  The Gambia actually broke ties with Taiwan in 2013, but Beijing refused to normalize ties with Banjul until March 2016. The Gambia's case also shows that some countries may break ties with Taipei *in expectation* of being rewarded by Beijing, as opposed to doing so *in response* to China providing them with material incentives. The authors thank Bonnie Glaser for suggesting this insight.

[4]  In the case of the Dominican Republic (which broke ties with Taiwan on May 1, 2018), China reportedly offered US$3.1 billion in investments and loans to de-recognize Taipei; Panama, which severed relations with Taiwan on June 12, 2017, switched to China after receiving a series of large-scale real-estate and port-development investments with the promise of further such inflows of foreign direct investment in the future (Yu and Blanchard, 2018; Reuters, 2017; Cole, 2017; Blanchard, 2017; Horton, 2018b).

[5]  On PADF generally, see PADF, undated(b); on PADF's work with Taiwan specifically, see PADF, undated(c).

[6]  Additionally, our search for available online public opinion or polling data on Taiwan's image in the LAC region did not turn up substantial reportable findings. We also considered approaching embassy staff from LAC countries with offices in the Washington, D.C., area, but found that the few representatives we reached out to were not able or willing to characterize their countries' relationship with or images of Taiwan. As such, most of our impressions of how Taiwan's aid is received in the region come from our engagements with international development specialists from the PADF, our conversations with U.S. officials and experts, and our reading of selected media reporting from the region. This could conceivably overstate or bias our impressions of how Taiwan's aid and assistance is perceived locally; such biases (if they exist), appear to be in the

no single national case can be considered entirely representative of other cases, our interviews with Taiwan and U.S. officials as well as international development specialists suggested that the selection of Honduras and Haiti were broadly applicable enough as to be generally valuable for developing insights into the lessons to be derived from Taiwan's broader aid and assistance programs in the LAC region.

Our research design drew on secondary and primary source literature related to Taiwan's foreign relations and international assistance programs (including in the two case study countries); China's foreign policy and foreign influence operations; and official U.S. government policy documents and statements. It also leveraged face-to-face and phone interviews with more than a dozen key U.S. and Taiwan officials and international development experts, as well as email exchanges with individuals involved in policymaking in both Washington and Taipei. At the conclusion of the study, we convened a roundtable discussion with eight subject-matter experts focused on Taiwan, U.S.-Asia policy, development, and the LAC region in RAND's Arlington, Virginia, offices to present our initial findings and elicit feedback.

## Why Study Taiwan's Development Assistance to Latin America and the Caribbean?

The questions at the heart of this study—Taiwan's development assistance to LAC nations and its impact on their decisions to maintain diplomatic ties with Taipei—matter to both Taiwan and the United States (as well as to the recipient countries in the region that benefit from the ROC's assistance programs). Recent research on Taiwan's overseas assistance programs has shown that "the enhancement of international status has continually been the most important determinant in Taiwan's foreign aid policy-making," a pattern that conforms with broader research in the field of political science that found "abundant statistical evidence that the donor's political interests, rather than general considerations of efficiency or the recipient countries' policies or needs, have dominated the donor countr[ies'] allocations of bilateral aid" (Lin and Lin, 2017). For Taiwan, the primary goal is to retain diplomatic recognition but also to ensure the ability to continue to participate in the widest variety of international fora as possible. As the "Foreign Policy Guidelines" listed on the website of the Ministry of Foreign Affairs (MOFA) clearly state, MOFA spares no effort "in implementing policies that enhance Taiwan's prosperity and promoting foreign relations that strengthen the international status of the ROC" as well as in "making concrete contributions to the global community, and enhancing its international profile through economic and humanitarian air policies" (Ministry of Foreign Affairs, Republic of China [Taiwan], 2016). These include direct government-to-government funding assistance and in-kind contributions, funding provided through international NGOs such as PADF, and support to civil society organizations and directly to local communities. In addition, since 1996, the Taiwan International Cooperation and Development Fund (ICDF), Taiwan's equivalent of the U.S. Agency for International

---

direction of aid being received positively rather than unfavorably. It is plausible to think that, to the extent local communities in the LAC region are aware of Taiwan, they see it as a developed, successful, and generous country that is offering them assistance without asking much in the way of costs. Interviewees we spoke with did say that Taiwan does a good job of publicizing its aid at the local level and strives to ensure that recipient communities know where it comes from; others stated that Taiwan's aid is positively regarded (even if the details of the Beijing-Taipei contest for diplomatic recognition are not understood or fully appreciated).

Development (USAID), has served as an important venue for assistance and outreach to Taiwan's developing nation diplomatic partners (ICDF, 2010). ICDF does this by focusing on "boosting socio-economic development, enhancing human resources and promoting economic relations," as well as offering "humanitarian assistance and provid[ing] aid in the event of natural disasters or international refugee crises" through "four core operations: lending and investment, technical cooperation, humanitarian assistance, and international education and training" (ICDF, undated[a]). Taiwan's reputation for generosity also stems from an extremely active set of corporate donors, civil society NGOs, and individual citizens who magnify the impact of its official state lending through their own giving and assistance (Lin and Lin, 2017). Such aid and assistance is largely relevant for the goal of retaining diplomatic recognition, although it may also create some spillover for the goal of enhancing or preserving Taiwan's ability to participate in international society and multinational organizations.

This report also describes U.S. efforts in the region to understand how Taiwan might achieve synergies with the United States in LAC-focused development assistance. Like Taiwan, the United States also pursues aid and assistance programs in Latin America and the Caribbean, while also paying close attention to the question of Taiwan's international status. Taiwan's aid and assistance programs to LAC nations cut across, affect, and are closely tracked by officials in the U.S. Department of State's Bureau of East Asia and the Pacific and its Bureau of Western Hemisphere Affairs, as well as USAID and representatives of the American Institute in Taiwan (Washington's unofficial organization for conducting contacts with Taipei). Members of academia, the think-tank community, and civil society organizations also follow Taiwan's participation in international society closely. Within the U.S. Congress, the ROC continues to have numerous supporters, with Senators Cory Gardner and Edward Markey of the Senate Foreign Relations Committee having introduced a bipartisan bill in May 2018, the Taiwan International Participation Act (TIPA) of 2018, to strengthen Taiwan's international standing (Gardner, 2018). Senators Gardner, Marco Rubio, Markey, and Bob Menendez followed up by introducing the Taiwan Allies International Protection and Enhancement Initiative (TAIPEI) Act in September 2018 to require the Executive Branch to put together a strategy "to engage with governments around the world to support Taiwan's diplomatic recognition or strengthen unofficial ties with Taiwan" ("U.S. Lawmakers Introduce TAIPEI Act," 2018).

Officially, the U.S. Department of State describes U.S. policy toward Taiwan as focused on supporting "Taiwan's membership in international organizations that do not require statehood as a condition of membership and encourag[ing] Taiwan's meaningful participation in international organizations where its membership is not possible" (U.S. Department of State, Bureau of East Asian and Pacific Affairs, 2018). The State Department's Bureau of Western Hemisphere Affairs, which focuses on the countries where Taiwan's aid to LAC countries ends up, works with partners throughout the Americas "to generate broad-based growth through freer trade and sound economic policies; to invest in the well-being of people from all walks of life; and to make democracy serve every citizen more effectively and justly" (U.S. Department of State, undated). While the State Department has overall responsibility for U.S. policy toward the region, it is not the only U.S. government agency focused on the issues under consideration here; in many ways, questions of development and disaster response lie at least as much in the purview of USAID, which has the lead for the twin missions of "ending extreme poverty and promoting the development of resilient, democratic societies that are able to realize their potential" (USAID, 2018a). Finally, because the United States does not maintain formal diplomatic ties with Taiwan, the American Institute in Taiwan (AIT) plays a role in coordinating "any programs, transactions, or other relations conducted or carried out by the President or any Agency of the United States Government with respect to Taiwan" (AIT, undated[b]). Thus, each of these institutions, and the United States as a whole, has an interest and equities at stake in Taiwan's aid and assistance programs, both for the impact of such programs on helping preserve Taiwan's meaningful participation in international society as well as delivering outcomes that improve the lives of people in the LAC region.[7]

With respect to preserving Taiwan's de facto independence and ability to preserve an international profile not defined by China, U.S. officials have privately sought to dissuade LAC nations from cutting ties with Taiwan and publicly encouraged "all concerned parties to engage in productive dialogue and to avoid escalatory or destabilizing moves" in the wake of Panama's severing of ties to Taipei (Lu, 2017). Similarly, in the wake of Burkina Faso's derecognition of Taiwan on May 24, 2018, the U.S. Department of State expressed "disappointment" in Ougadougou for cutting ties with Taipei ("U.S. Says It Is Disappointed with Burkina Faso Switch," 2018). And the White House Press Secretary issued a statement in the wake of El Salvador's decision to recognize Beijing by expressing Washington's "grave concern" and noting that the decision would result in "a reevaluation of our relationship with El Salvador" ("Statement from the Press Secretary on El Salvador," 2018). The White House also took the unprecedented step of recalling the U.S. ambassadors to the Dominican Republic, El Salvador, and Panama on September 7, 2018, "for consultations related to recent decisions [by those governments] to no longer recognize Taiwan" (Reuters, 2018).

Indeed, some analysts of the U.S.-Taiwan relationship believe that Taiwan has never had stronger allies in high-ranking policy positions in the U.S. government than it does under the Trump administration (RAND interview #7B). As the Congressional Research Service assessed in late 2018, the Trump administration "has viewed China's engagement in Latin America with more suspicion" than its predecessors, partly owing to Beijing's "apparent goal" of trying to "isolate Taiwan by attempting to lure away Latin American and Caribbean countries that still maintain diplomatic relations" with Taipei (Sullivan and Lum, 2018; Koleski and Blivas, 2018).[8] Senior U.S. leaders' remarks support the view that the Trump administration is prioritizing cooperation with Taiwan more highly and regarding China more skeptically than previous administrations. For example, Secretary of State Mike Pompeo, in a major policy speech on the Trump administration's Indo-Pacific strategy, specifically praised Taiwan's development experience, noting that, in Taiwan, "economic development went hand-in-hand with creating an open, democratic society that blossomed into a high-tech powerhouse" (Pompeo, 2018). Similarly, Vice President Mike Pence, in remarks on the administration's U.S.-China policy delivered at the Hudson Institute on October 4, 2018, commented that

---

[7] Additionally, U.S. policy under the Trump administration has sought to dramatically curtail the arrival of immigrants and asylum seekers from Central America and the Caribbean, with Haiti and Honduras specifically singled out. As such, an additional interest of the current U.S. administration in Taiwan's aid to the region includes the creation of better living conditions in Haiti and Honduras that could reduce incentives for people from these countries to seek to move to the United States (see Caldwell, 2018; Davis, Stolberg, and Kaplan, 2018). At the same time, as subject-matter experts we spoke with noted, the U.S. image in Latin America and the Caribbean has been in decline as a consequence of the Trump administration's policies on aid, trade, and immigration, which could make it more attractive and effective for Taiwan to coordinate its aid strategy toward the LAC region with the U.S. quietly rather than publicly for some time to come (RAND interviews #7B and #7D).

[8] Koleski and Blivas also take note of China's efforts to purloin Taiwan's diplomatic partnerships in the LAC region in their review of issues related to China's growing regional influence that are concerning for the United States.

"America will always believe Taiwan's embrace of democracy shows a better path for all the Chinese people" (Pence, 2018).

At the same time, U.S. observers worry that, at some point, if further erosion of the ROC's international recognition occurs, pressures might grow inside Taiwan to abandon the ROC as an identity and seek to redefine the nation's public face as "Taiwan," a move that China might treat as a casus belli. In addition, the severing of the ROC's diplomatic partnerships in Latin America and the Caribbean puts at risk Taiwan's ability to engage in "stopover diplomacy," whereby the ROC president's plane touches down in the United States for refueling, providing an opportunity for limited but politically meaningful contact between U.S. nationals and ROC officials.

Reflecting these long-standing U.S. interests in and commitments to Taiwan's security, autonomy, and international role, on March 21, 2018, U.S. Deputy Assistant Secretary of State Alex Wong visited Taiwan, where he described "the aim of U.S. policy [as ensuring] that Taiwan's people can continue along their chosen path, free from coercion," including the psychological and diplomatic pressure stemming from China's efforts to isolate Taiwan internationally (Horton, 2018a). Echoing these comments, on April 23, 2018, AIT director Kin Moy reiterated the support of the United States for Taiwan's participation in international society, most notably as an observer at the annual World Health Assembly (WHA), the decisionmaking body of the World Health Organization (WHO) (Taipei Times, 2018[a]). Katina Adams, spokesperson for the Bureau of East Asian and Pacific Affairs at the Department of State, described Taiwan as a "force for good in the world" in an email exchange with reporters on April 28, 2018, reiterating the U.S. support for Taiwan's meaningful participation and membership in international organizations that do not require statehood, such as the International Civil Aviation Organization and the WHA/WHO (Lu and Hsiao, 2018).

LAC region countries and peoples that receive Taiwan's aid and assistance have perhaps the greatest stake in continuing to partner with the ROC on issues of development, resilience, and recovery. Data from the PADF, Taiwan's ICDF, and other sources show that, across Belize, El Salvador, Guatemala, Haiti, Honduras, Nicaragua, Paraguay, the Federation of St. Christopher and Nevis, St. Lucia, and Saint Vincent and the Grenadines, communities that have received aid from Taiwan have seen their agricultural outputs rise; food consumption and food security grow; incomes increase; resilience to flooding, earthquakes, and extreme weather events improve; and have recovered faster after disaster struck (PADF, 2016; ICDF, undated[e], undated[f], and interviewees' remarks in conversations conducted for this project). The fact that the ROC itself has achieved such spectacular economic development—while located in an area where earthquakes, typhoons, and other natural disasters and tragedies are all too common—provides Taiwan with the ability to inspire, assist, empathize, and cooperate on issues with partners on which it has relevant experiences to draw from and use to tailor its resilience and recovery strategies. Interviewees often commented on how Taiwan's approach to aid leverages not only official government funds but does so in a way that is accountable; is responsive to recipient countries' concerns and interests; works to develop genuine, long-term partnerships that empower local communities and individuals; and is effectively bolstered by Taiwan's private-sector giving by corporations, foundations, civil society, academic institutions, and official giving directed through multilateral institutions such as PADF (among others) (RAND interviews with regional development assistant experts).

We conclude that, conceived of solely on its own terms, Taiwan's development assistance is valuable for convincing countries not to break ties with Taipei in favor of Beijing. Such aid, however, must be situated in and bolstered by Taiwan's broader trade, investment, debt financing, political, military-to-military, and historical relationships with recipient countries. Other important factors include the state of these countries' ties with the United States and the recipient countries' identities, norms, histories, and the policy goals of their current leaders. These findings are broadly consonant with other experts' research on Taiwan's diplomatic relationships with the region.[9] As one U.S. interviewee stated, alone, "Taiwan's spending programs probably make a marginal difference on recipient nations' decisions about recognition." Instead, it is more likely that "the deep history of the two countries' bilateral relations—a shared sense of common identity [as democratic nations] and/or a concern about Chinese influence—probably best explains why some countries don't switch recognition to Beijing" (RAND interview #6B).[10]

At the same time, it is worth bearing in mind that the PRC appears likely to continue expending substantial resources to poach Taiwan diplomatic partnerships, and even generous giving focused on empowering recipient communities as true partners can at times be trumped by Beijing's deeper pockets or the idiosyncratic calculations of aid recipients and diplomatic partners. Beijing's announcement that its Belt and Road Initiative includes the LAC region signals that China will continue to commit resources to poach Taiwan's diplomatic partners.

Additionally, no single factor can predict when or why countries will change, although aid (gifts, grants, or loans), trade, and investment are widely believed to be the most critical factors. As one analysis of Taiwan's use of foreign aid has argued, foreign aid may not serve as a guarantee against de-recognition and ostracism, but "foreign aid on a shoestring—amid China's counter-aid diplomacy—[is a] foolproof recipe for deepening Taipei's diplomatic isolation" (Tubilewicz and Guilloux, 2011). For these reasons, Taipei will likely need to both maintain a substantial commitment to using foreign aid as a diplomatic tool and harbor a measure of caution and develop a fallback plan—or perhaps even a proactive strategy—for dealing with the fallout of the further loss of diplomatic recognition from its current partners. An expert who has looked at the issue of Taipei's public diplomacy contest with Beijing in Central America has argued that, ultimately, "public diplomacy is not an equalizer between nation-states of vastly different sizes when the smaller nation-state is constrained by a lack of widespread diplomatic recognition" (Alexander, 2014, p. 198).

Taiwan has run substantial aid and assistance programs in the LAC region, and previous studies concluded that these programs have been "indispensable" to the ROC's quest to retain diplomatic partners in the region (Erikson and Chen, 2007; Council on Hemispheric Affairs, 2008).[11] Aid has continued at substantial levels in recent years; in 2010, Taiwan's foreign assistance was US$438 million; 2012, US$332 million; 2013, US$299 million; and 2015, US$290 million (all in constant 2018 U.S. dollars [US$]; 2015 was the last year for which full data were available) (Ministry of Foreign Affairs, Republic of China [Taiwan], 2012, 2014,

---

[9]  Research by Erikson and Chen (2007), as well as later work by Rich and Dahmer (2017), highlighted Taiwan's substantial trade and investment advantages over China, as well as the identity and diplomatic norms held by Central American nations, as critical factors in explaining why these countries have not switched recognition to Beijing.

[10]  Tubilewicz and Guilloux (2011) similarly find that shared democratic identity and norms play a role in helping explain the persistence of Latin American countries' diplomatic recognition of the ROC.

[11]  Indeed, Tubilewicz and Guilloux (2011) argue that, contra the widespread impression that the Chen Shui-bian administration lost diplomatic allies despite spending heavily on foreign aid, it actually lost them because it did not spend as much as it was accused of spending by the Kuomintang during that party's time in opposition.

2015).[12] In the LAC region specifically, Taiwan contributed an estimated 20 percent of Haiti's government budget in the late 2000s (Rich, 2010), reportedly gave more than US$232 million in loans and grants to Honduras in the 2010s (Menchu, 2017), offered US$600 million in aid and concessionary loans to Guatemala, US$60 million in gifts and loans to Belize in 2017 (Ramos, 2017), and provided millions of dollars to El Salvador for disaster relief (some of which are alleged to have been diverted to former President Francisco Flores's personal bank account), to list just a few concrete details (Malkin, 2017).

If diplomatic recognition is to represent anything more than a mere repeated tax on Taiwan's citizenry by foreign governments who can extract it in exchange for short-term recognition, however, it must be supported by more than just cash and aid transfers from Taipei to lower-income recipient nations. The broader relationships and goodwill that Taiwan's assistance is intended to develop through well-tailored development assistance and educational training, as well as disaster preparedness and relief, carry a strong logic that embeds them in a set of ties that complicate any attempt by Beijing to simply deliver bags of cash to foreign leaders in exchange for dropping recognition of Taipei. One interviewee noted:

> Taiwan's aid is 'sticky'—it leads to long-term relationships, and these are important in Latin America. [The more they interact, the more] regional partners [come to] see Taiwan's development as miraculous and its vulnerabilities to natural disasters as similar, leading to a sense of kinship. [Taiwan] strives to convey to [its] aid recipients that sustainable development requires a long-term partnership and that cooperation with Taiwan leads to the empowerment of local communities. (RAND interview #2A)

## Organization of This Report

Chapter Two describes Taiwan's aid and assistance programs to Latin America and the Caribbean, focusing in particular on the ROC's economic aid and assistance with resilience and disaster relief in Honduras and Haiti. We present information about the types of contributions Taiwan has made to these partner nations as well as how the aid is delivered. Chapter Three presents an examination of U.S. aid and assistance to Honduras and Haiti and U.S. perspectives on Taiwan's role in the LAC region, drawn from insights from interviews with U.S. interlocutors about how Taiwan might be able to increase synergies with U.S. giving in the region while also further incentivizing LAC countries not to switch diplomatic recognition to China. Chapter Four offers some concluding thoughts on how Taiwan can best think about and leverage its aid and assistance programs and points to potential further questions for research.

---

[12] Unless otherwise stated, all dollar amounts are in U.S. dollars. Taiwan does not appear to have published an annual white paper on its overseas development assistance in 2011, nor does any report appear to have been published since 2015.

# CHAPTER TWO

# Understanding Taiwan's Aid and Assistance to Latin America and the Caribbean

Since the mid-1990s, Taiwan has played a significant role in providing aid and assistance to countries in the LAC region. Taiwan's aid and assistance programs, generally divided between technical assistance intended to raise agricultural output and community resilience and recovery aid programs that are intended to mitigate disasters such as earthquakes and typhoons, are generally seen as ways to incentivize Taiwan's diplomatic partners to retain their diplomatic ties with Taipei. While globally, 21 of the 24 countries receiving assistance from Taiwan in 2014 were diplomatic partners of the ROC, the figure for the LAC region was 12 out of 12, signaling the critical role that aid and assistance have played in Taiwan's efforts to maintain its international standing in the world through assistance to partners in that region.[1] This chapter provides a broad overview of the ways in which Taiwan has provided assistance to countries in the region, while also competing against China for diplomatic recognition there; it then turns to a more in-depth description of two specific cases, Haiti and Honduras.

## Comparative Description of Chinese and Taiwanese Engagement in Latin America and the Caribbean

As a starting point, we present a brief comparative baseline description of China's aid, trade, and investments in Latin America and the Caribbean, since these are in part what Taiwan seeks to benchmark its own efforts against. While we had hoped to be able to provide a comprehensive picture of Chinese economic contacts with the LAC region, such information unfortunately does not appear to be available in the open-source domain. Available PRC government documents, open media reporting, and expert analyses nonetheless suggest that China has, since issuing its first policy paper on China and the LAC region in 2008, devoted growing attention to, and consequently expanded its economic contacts and influence in, the LAC region (Ministry of Foreign Affairs of the People's Republic of China, 2016; Campbell and Valette, 2014). Senior Chinese officials, including Hu Jintao and Xi Jinping, have visited the region regularly over the past decade. Separately, while comprehensive data on Chinese aid and trade were not available, LAC exports to China reportedly experienced a 30 percent increase in 2017 (Inter-American Development Bank, 2017). China has invested heavily in highway construction in Jamaica (it built a US$720 million north-south highway) and port infrastructure in the Bahamas (the PRC also built a casino and luxury hotel complex), as well

---

[1] Data on 2014 recipients are reported in Lin and Lin (2017).

as other forms of lending to regional partners. Much of this has been supported by Chinese development financing to the region; while such funding reportedly dropped in 2017, it still came in at US$9 billion, and total lending has topped US$150 billion since 2005, according to one recent analysis (Myers and Gallagher, 2018).[2] Indeed, according to Maggiorelli (2017), preferential loans have long been the predominant form of Chinese aid to the LAC region. In addition, Beijing established the China–Community of Latin America and the Caribbean States Forum and recently announced that its Belt and Road Initiative will be extended to the region. Collectively, such developments have led analysts to characterize China as "making inroads" or "filling the void" left by declining U.S. and European attention to the LAC region (Southerland, 2017; Tannenbaum, 2018).

For its part, most of Taiwan's aid and assistance to the LAC region comes in the form of direct assistance. One interviewee with knowledge of Taiwan's giving characterized direct assistance as constituting as much as 90 percent of Taiwan's overall aid—with the remaining 10 percent broken down to about 8–9 percent funneled through the ICDF and the remaining roughly 1–2 percent transferred through other organizations, such as the PADF (RAND interview #2). Unfortunately, data on the exact breakdown of Taiwan's assistance by modality (direct versus via ICDF versus via other international NGOs) proved difficult to obtain.[3] This chapter focuses on initiatives carried out by the ICDF within Taiwan's overall development assistance strategy. We supplement the discussion with broader data from Taiwan's self-reporting on assistance to the region through other modalities as well as open-source media and discussions with development experts at the PADF. We also evaluate economic assistance and disaster relief projects in Honduras and Haiti as case studies for understanding Taiwan's aid, using these to explore dimensions of Taiwan's assistance programs while recognizing that no two cases can fully reflect the variety of the other LAC countries Taiwan gives aid to. By examining these cases in greater detail, this chapter lays the foundation for a discussion in Chapter Three, which focuses on how Taiwan's giving overlaps with U.S. assistance and how U.S. observers see Taiwan's role in the LAC region.

## International Cooperation and Development Fund

ICDF is the main government agency in Taiwan in charge of planning, executing, and monitoring development aid programs abroad and is the central conduit for Taiwan's official development assistance. ICDF is headquartered in Taipei and has 112 employees in Taiwan and 150 staff stationed at missions overseas (ICDF, undated[a]). As then-ICDF Secretary-General Tao Wen-lung related in a 2012 interview, ICDF's mission is to "promote humanitarianism, economic progress and sustainable development while advancing Taiwan's diplomatic interests," an approach it pursues through programs and practices that have evolved to be "in line with contemporary international development assistance norms," including the use of performance

---

[2]  Note that the majority of the lending that Myers and Gallagher document relates to countries in South America that are not included in the definition of the LAC region used in this report.

[3]  A review of ICDF's sources of funding, when compared with MOFA's reporting on annual overall funding levels, suggests that the figures reported here are approximately accurate. In 2016, ICDF reports being funded and commissioned by MOFA to execute projects focused on technical cooperation at the level of New Taiwan (NT) $1.15B (US$38.2 million) as part of an overall Taiwan overseas development assistance budget of NT$9.76 billion (US$324.5 million), a ratio of roughly 11.8 percent (or slightly more than the interviewee's estimated 8–9 percent) (ICDF, undated[c]).

metrics, local buy-in, transfer of successful programs to local stakeholders, and termination of projects that do not deliver results on time or on budget (Her, 2012).

To carry out its mission, ICDF operates four core departments: (1) lending and investment, (2) technical cooperation, (3) humanitarian assistance, and (4) international education and training. Lending and investment is the most direct form of aid and involves the lending of funds to regional lending institutions or the recipient country for specific poverty alleviation or governance purpose. Technical cooperation, on the other hand, involves cooperation and coordination in which technical expertise or materials are provided by Taiwan to an intermediary in the recipient country. In contrast with lending and investment, technical cooperation involves some sort of partner arrangement with local institutions for knowledge transfer within the recipient country. Humanitarian assistance is a narrower form of aid and involves the provision of resources or knowledge for natural disaster prevention or alleviation. Finally, international education and training generally involves exchanges between an entity based in Taiwan and an entity receiving direct educational instruction in the recipient country. Together, these four departments support aid projects in areas such as environmental protection, public health, agriculture, education, and information and communications technology, among others.

ICDF generally offers funding to recipient countries through direct or indirect investments and financial lending operations whose revenues are used to support bilateral or multilateral technical cooperation projects, humanitarian assistance operations, and education and training programs. ICDF often works closely with local partners and lending institutions to ensure its assistance meets the needs of foreign countries. Organizationally, ICDF retains close ties with the Taiwan MOFA. For example, Joseph Wu, the current chair of ICDF, is also the Minister of Foreign Affairs of Taiwan (ICDF, undated[b]).

## ICDF's Role in Latin America

Latin America is one of the largest markets for ICDF funds. In total, ICDF has dispersed more than US$152 million in development funds over the past 15 years (ICDF, undated[d]).[4] Of the 159 projects within these seven countries, lending and investment makes up the lion's share of aid modalities at 47 percent, while technical cooperation, humanitarian assistance, and international education make up 40 percent, 13 percent, and less than 1 percent, respectively. Historically, lending and investment has been the preferred mode of development aid. However, the large portion of technical cooperation (40 percent) reflects a growing awareness among donor countries around the world of adopting a "needs-based aid architecture" built on partnerships among donors and recipients that are aligned with sustainable development goals of a country, as opposed to the more transactional modality of lending and investment (United Nations, 2010).

Through the provision of aid, ICDF seeks to boost economic development and social welfare outcomes across a range of categories. These categories match the needs of most countries in Latin America and the Caribbean and reflect investments in industries that LAC nations prioritize, including agriculture, microfinance for small and medium enterprises

---

[4]  ICDF's focus in these seven countries is not a coincidence. They all maintain formal diplomatic relations with Taiwan. ICDF funding tends to follow the diplomatic recognition of the ROC. This is supported in the case of the Caribbean as well.

(SMEs), information technology, health care, and disaster preparedness and relief. With the exception of disaster preparedness, which will be addressed later in the chapter, each of these sectors and ICDF's contribution to them are highlighted in the next sections.

### Enabling Sustainable, Profitable Agriculture

Agriculture remains one of the most important industries in Latin America. Coffee, bananas, sugar cane, beef, and poultry products represent traditional staples in Latin America and are some of its most important exports. The reduction of export quotas among many countries in Latin America in tandem with increasing competition from agricultural product imports, however, has stunted economic growth in recent years (Morgan, 2017). To prevent this situation from deteriorating further, ICDF has launched several agricultural projects to raise the international competitiveness of local products. Given geographic and climate advantages as well as the region's proximity to North American markets, ICDF has sought to promote diversification of crops by introducing high-yield crop technology, marketing functions, and food-processing innovations that have allowed local SME farms to move up the value chain. For example, technical missions in Belize, the Dominican Republic, Guatemala, Costa Rica, and Panama carry out food-processing projects, providing technology and credits for local cooperatives and farmer associations to process fruits (ICDF, undated[d]). In Panama, Honduras, and Paraguay, products from small farm holders have been marketed to centralized markets and supermarkets to reduce transport and marketing costs and increase income (ICDF, undated[d]). An agricultural revitalization credit project is being staged in Nicaragua to help farmers reduce production costs, expand local and foreign markets, and take advantage of their local natural resources effectively (ICDF, undated[d]). Another technical cooperation project in Nicaragua focuses on improving horticultural crop production by promoting the grading and packing of produce and as well as developing demonstration plots of swine and rice (ICDF, undated[d]).

### Promoting Small and Medium Enterprise Development Through Microfinance

With increasing global economic integration over the past three decades, SME development is one of the focal points within the Latin American region. Drawing on Taiwan's own success in developing SMEs, ICDF has provided guidance and consultancy services to enterprises across Latin America to promote industrial transformation. ICDF does so by providing microcredit to assist SMEs in obtaining necessary funds to develop and increase competitiveness. At the broadest level, ICDF has several intraregional microfinance arrangements that extend funds to regional development banks that then lend to local SMEs. One example of this arrangement is the Specialized Financial Intermediary Development Fund—Próspero Microfinanzas Fund (PMF), in which ICDF contributes funds to the Inter-American Development Bank, which then invests in microfinance institutions in Latin America (ICDF, undated[d]). PMF is responsible for identifying and managing the subprojects. The goal is to make equity investments in SMEs in Latin America to create a more competitive microfinance industry, as well as to expand underserved markets of strategic interest for countries in the region (ICDF, undated[d]).

Another key intraregional lending institution that ICDF works closely with in Latin America is the Central American Bank for Economic Integration (CABEI). For example, ICDF initiated a region-wide rural infrastructure–lending project that commits loans to CABEI, which then relends to rural associations, such as the Honduran Social Investment

Fund (Fondo Hondureño de Inversión Social); that organization then uses the funds to build roads, water-treatment plants, and sanitation and electrical facilities (ICDF, undated[d]).

Finally, ICDF uses credit and training projects to assist vocational schools, enabling them to train personnel in such skills as production technology, operations management, marketing, and factory consultation services. For example, the SME Development Project in Guatemala assists SMEs by performing site visits and providing technical assistance and consultancy services (ICDF, undated[d]). The Taiwan Investment and Trade Service Mission in Central America partnered with the Ministry of Economy of the Republic of Guatemala and Rafael Landívar University to execute the project. Training courses included handcrafted wood furniture, agribusiness, human resource management, and business management (ICDF, undated[d]).

## Boosting Information Technology Education and Skills

For strong economic growth to be maintained, the private sector must take advantage of digital opportunities and know-how. As one of the most developed markets for information technology (IT) in the world, Taiwan has a deep knowledge base to draw from (Khan, 2004). ICDF leverages Taiwan's unique experience in this domain to help reduce the digital divide by providing IT hardware and software to countries throughout Latin America and regularly hosting training seminars to build human capital. ICDF also works alongside educational institutions to share its own developmental experiences. One project in Guatemala trains students and professionals in IT-related enterprise management by developing software, offering classes in IT development, and advising the Guatemalan National Council of Science and Technology on investment strategies in the local IT industry (ICDF, undated[d]). Another IT-focused project in Guatemala set up in 2008 established a fund to finance student loan programs in eligible technological education and vocational training institutions. For this project, CABEI managed the funds provided by ICDF. ICDF also funds students in Latin America to study in Taiwan and improve their IT skills. For one project, ICDF cooperated with the University of Maryland, the Organization of American States, and the Young Americas Business Trust to host the Talent and Innovation Competition of the Americas in Taipei (ICDF, undated[d]). Teams of students from across Latin America competed in developing business plans, filming a promotional video, and designing a website in their chosen industry. Winning teams were awarded scholarships and access to IT networks in Taiwan.

## Raising Health Care Standards and Awareness

Taiwan has also assisted countries in the LAC region by extending funding and support for access to affordable health care. Taiwan's health care sector is among the best in the world, and ICDF leverages this when it extends development assistance. Much of Taiwan's medical support is organized in cooperation with the International Health Care Strategic Alliance (IHCSA)—a coalition that brings together ICDF and 37 Taiwan hospitals and medical institutions to provide countries in Latin America with a range of medical aid and services. Mobile medical missions are a key part of this support; ICDF has organized more than 80 missions to Honduras, El Salvador, Nicaragua, Guatemala, and Paraguay in cooperation with the IHCSA, setting up temporary clinics in urban and rural communities and providing care to locals (ICDF, undated[d]). Doctors from Taiwan provide direct medical care as well as work with local medical professionals to raise awareness on contagious and communicable disease prevention (ICDF, undated[d]). ICDF also funds short-term medical training scholarships for doctors from around the world, supporting them to visit Taiwan and participate in hospital residency programs. Programs last one to three months; the project has been in operation since 2016 (ICDF, undated[d]).

## ICDF's Role in the Caribbean

The Caribbean relies on a narrower range of industries than does Latin America for economic development and has a much lower economic base (Morgan, 2017). Agriculture and tourism comprise the backbone of economic activity for most countries in the region. These industries are highly vulnerable to the adverse effects of climate change, such as the intensification and frequency of extreme weather events and subsequent environmental degradation, which directly affect industry revenues by impacting crop yields and tourism arrivals. Compared with Latin America, however, farming has greater limitations and higher costs in the Caribbean, since most countries are island nations where shipping and logistics cost are comparatively high (Nicholson, 2015). The main export crops are bananas and sugar cane, although many countries would like to diversify into other crops, enhance their production capacity, and climb the value-added ladder. As a result, ICDF has designed microcredit projects for many Caribbean nations to assist farmers in acquiring production equipment to boost output.

ICDF has a presence in five Caribbean countries, including St. Lucia, St. Vincent and the Grenadines, St. Kitts and Nevis, Haiti, and the Dominican Republic. Of the 66 ICDF-funded projects carried out in these countries over the last 15 years, technical cooperation constituted the majority of aid modalities at 66 percent, while humanitarian assistance, lending and investment, and international education and training made up 24 percent, 4.5 percent, and 4.5 percent, respectively (ICDF, undated[d]). Within technical cooperation, the majority of ICDF projects focus on disaster preparedness, agriculture, health care, and governance issues. Within humanitarian assistance, the majority of projects focused on disaster relief and infrastructure construction. The next section explores Taiwan's aid and assistance to Honduras and Haiti as specific cases.

## ICDF Assistance with Disaster Preparedness in Haiti and Honduras

The Caribbean is one of the most disaster-prone areas in the world (Fagen, 2008). Natural events such as droughts, hurricanes, and flash floods have caused significant and recurrent damage to livelihoods, the environment, infrastructure, and the economy in recent years, and the situation is only expected to worsen as the effects of climate change become more severe (Jones, 2016). Latin America, while not suffering from the scale and scope of natural disasters that afflict the Caribbean, is still vulnerable to destructive weather events. As the January 2018 magnitude 7.6 earthquake that struck off the Caribbean coast of Honduras and the 7.0 earthquake that struck Haiti in 2010 make clear, the LAC region is also exposed to the threat of extreme geological events. With the assistance of Taiwan, Haiti and Honduras have received rapid delivery of aid during crises and invested in risk-reduction initiatives to help prepare for future calamities.

### Haiti

Over one-quarter of all ICDF projects in Haiti go toward humanitarian assistance–based projects following a major natural disaster or technical cooperation–based projects to support resiliency and disaster preparedness efforts during non–natural disaster periods. These projects address the fact that Haiti has fallen victim to some of the worst natural disasters in the region over the past decade. Two events in particular—the magnitude 7.0 earthquake near Port-au-Prince in January 2010 and Hurricane Sandy in 2012—devastated roads, bridges, and buildings across the country and displaced millions of Haitians (Kang, 2016). Taiwan provided assistance in response to both of these tragedies, sending desperately needed food, supplies, and reconstruction assistance.

#### *Cash-for-Work Relief and Recovery for Haiti*

Following the January 2010 earthquake, ICDF partnered with Mercy Corps—a U.S.-based NGO—to initiate transition from immediate emergency response efforts to short- to medium-term economic recovery through a cash-for-work program (ICDF, undated[d]). This initiative provided assistance for the cleanup process while providing displaced citizens with cash to address their own immediate needs, increasing the flow of money back into the local economy. This project resulted in the provision of daily wages for at least 500 Haitians working an average of 30 days each on community-identified recovery projects such as clearing debris and construction of temporary community living facilities. ICDF funds also assisted in the creation of ten community "tool banks" for use in debris-removal projects (ICDF, undated[d]).

#### *Haiti Earthquake Emergency Material Delivery Project*

ICDF cooperated with World Vision—a U.S.-based Christian humanitarian aid NGO—to send 105 tons of emergency materials to Haiti. Materials included tents, instant food rations, water purification equipment, and family hygiene kits (ICDF, undated[d]).

#### *Haiti Earthquake Medical Mission*

The ICDF partnered with the Taiwan Root Medical Peace Corps, MOFA, and the Taiwan Department of Health to send a medical mission to Port-au-Prince to aid sick and injured Haitians after the January 2010 earthquake. ICDF also contributed US$134,000 to cover the expenses of 42 medical staff from Taiwan. The mission treated more than 10,000 people (ICDF, undated[d]).

#### *Haiti Earthquake Rice Donation Project*

In coordination with the Taiwan Agriculture and Food Agency and the Taiwanese NGO Food for the Poor, ICDF delivered 200 tons of rice to Port-au-Prince following the January 2010 earthquake (ICDF, undated[d]).

#### *Haiti Earthquake Calamity Recovery Assistance Project*

ICDF worked with Haiti's Ministry of Agriculture, Natural Resources and Rural Development to provide post-disaster assistance following the January 2010 earthquake. This long-term project sought to revive the agricultural sector by resettling survivors of the earthquake and increasing the income available to farmers by offering training in auxiliary occupations, such as construction (ICDF, undated[d]).

### Haiti New Hope Village Residents Resettlement Project

After the 2010 earthquake, ICDF and MOFA invested in a multistage project called the New Hope Village Resettlement Project to build a relocation village in Savane Diane (ICDF, undated[d]). The village relocated displaced Haitians from Port-au-Prince and initiated a series of projects to provide food, shelter, and retraining in basic skills for employment.[5]

### Emergency Cholera Prevention and Response for Households Affected by Hurricane Sandy

This project sought to contribute to cholera prevention following outbreaks in Haiti, the Dominican Republic, and other Caribbean nations as a result of Hurricane Sandy in 2012. ICDF worked with World Vision in Haiti to provide highly vulnerable populations with prepositioned cholera supplies, oral rehydration points, and water purification units (ICDF, undated[d]). ICDF and World Vision worked closely with local Haitian authorities such as the Direction Sanitaire du Centre of Haiti, the Ministère de la Santé Publique et de la Population (Ministry of Public Health and Population), and the Direction Nationale de l'Eau Potable et de l'Assainissement (National Directorate for Potable Water and Sanitation), as well as with international agencies such as the WHO and the Pan-American Health Organization to coordinate the project (ICDF, undated[d]). The project was able to reach at least 220,000 patients in Haiti.

### Disaster Preparedness and Mitigation Project in the Southeast Department of Haiti and the Border Region of the Dominican Republic

Taiwan and the ICDF have also worked with international NGOs such as the PADF to help Haiti deal with disasters before they occur. Since 2012, the Taiwan PADF Disaster Assistance and Reconstruction Fund for Latin America and the Caribbean has extended at least US$2.5 million in humanitarian assistance and disaster recovery facilities, with the aim of helping at least 500,000 people recover from the effects of natural disasters and climate change (PADF, 2016). One example is a project called the Disaster Preparedness and Mitigation Project in the Southeast Department of Haiti and the Border Region of the Dominican Republic. This project sought to combine high-technology innovation with low-technology solutions to reduce the negative impact of natural disasters on communities in southeast Haiti and on the southeast border region between Haiti and the Dominican Republic (PADF, 2013a, p. 1). The project was a close collaboration with Haiti's Department of Civil Protection and its civil-protection structures to improve synergies between the various actors in disaster response and mitigation. The project reinforced the capacity of the local civil-protection committees to respond to disasters through information sharing, targeted training, and communication channels among local areas, mayors' offices, and national-level leadership. The ROC government and ICDF contributed US$300,000 to the project (PADF, 2013a, p. 34).

### Honduras

While Honduras has not suffered as many natural disasters as Haiti in recent years, it too faces threats including floods, hurricanes, earthquakes, and drought. ICDF has launched several projects to help the government of Honduras withstand such events and prepare for calamities in the future.

---

[5]  The ICDF produced a promotional video that publicized the achievements of these six projects (ICDF, 2014).

### Capability Enhancement in Using Geographic Information Systems

The governments of Nicaragua, Honduras, and El Salvador sought technical cooperation with Taiwan to enhance their monitoring and governance capacity during natural disasters and crises (ICDF, undated[d]). The specific aim of the project was to introduce geographic information systems (GIS) technology to improve the respective country's access to satellite imaging and technical capacity, which proved to be a key constraint on the countries' ability to react effectively during natural disasters. The project adopted a region-wide approach toward implementation by strengthening environmental monitoring of key protected areas and nature reserves through satellite imagery to better understand changes in topography, upgrading the technical capacity of GIS operations through training and technology transfer, and using satellite imagery to enhance environmental management (ICDF, undated[d]). ICDF worked closely with the Honduran National Institute of Forest Conservation and Development, Protected Areas and Wildlife; the Ministry of Energy, Natural Resources, Environment and Mining; Permanent Contingency Commission; and the National Autonomous Water and Sewer Service. ICDF contributed US$1 million to the project (ICDF, undated[d]).

### Housing Solidarity Reconstruction Program

Two million people in Honduras were affected by Hurricane Mitch in 1998, with at least 427,000 temporarily placed in shelters (ICDF, undated[d]). The primary objective of the Housing Solidarity Reconstruction Program was to rebuild houses in areas of higher elevation for about 2,000 families in most immediate need of land and housing. ICDF worked closely with the Secretary of Public Works, Transportation and Housing of the Republic of Honduras and contributed US$6 million to the project (ICDF, undated[d]).

### Neighborhood-Based Approach to Disaster Risk Reduction for Communities in Tegucigalpa

Honduras has a large number of informal urban settlements near the capital of Tegucigalpa. Were a natural disaster to hit this area, tens of thousands of citizens would be vulnerable to landslides and floods. To increase the resilience of vulnerable populations, ICDF funded a 13-month project implemented by the PADF. The project benefited more than 12,200 people (PADF, 2013b, p. 3).

## Conclusion: The Impact of Taiwan's Regional Assistance in Latin America and the Caribbean

As this review makes clear, through its aid programs, Taiwan has given numerous communities in the LAC region an opportunity to improve farming outcomes and ensure greater resistance to damaging crop diseases, among other development outcomes. Likewise, the ROC has also assisted regional partner nations in preparing for, responding to, and recovering from natural disasters and outbreaks of infectious disease. What is less clear is the extent to which such aid and assistance affects recipient nations' leaders' decisions about whether or not to maintain formal diplomatic relations with Taipei. Translating the goodwill that assistance generates at the local level into senior leadership commitment to retain ties is not an automatic process, but one that requires a mix of careful messaging intended to build durable grassroots and elite support. As one interviewee for this study noted, Taiwan needs to walk a fine line in its giving programs, focusing on the "quality of aid and striving to help its diplomatic partners without appearing transactional" to avoid creating a moral hazard whereby countries can continually threaten to abandon Taipei to extract more assistance as the price for maintaining ties (RAND interview #2). Colin R. Alexander, in his 2014 study of Taiwan's public diplomacy in Central America, has similarly warned that Taiwan needs to improve its focus on messaging to the publics in the region, not just elites, lest Taiwan's "overwhelming, explicit, single-purpose foreign policy [goal of seeking to retain diplomatic recognition come to be seen as implying that] Taiwan's national interests must come first and [its] image cultivation toward the Central American public [be seen as] secondary" (Alexander, 2014, p. 10). Chapter Three describes how the ROC's giving fits with U.S. policy priorities for Taiwan and the LAC region and how U.S. officials and observers see Taiwan's role in the region.

# U.S. Aid to Latin America and the Caribbean and U.S. Views of Taiwan's Role in the Region

## U.S. Aid to Latin America and the Caribbean

The United States provides substantial official assistance to countries in the Western hemisphere, with Haiti and Honduras among the most prominent recipients of U.S. aid. This chapter presents a review of U.S. assistance to these two countries and reports on U.S. officials' perceptions of the role of Taiwan's aid programs in the LAC region. We highlight areas where Taiwan could adjust its own assistance programs to better align with U.S. aid to achieve synergies while also potentially creating stronger incentives for countries in the LAC region that might contemplate switching diplomatic recognition to Beijing to remain with Taipei.

Official U.S. assistance to the LAC region comes from a variety of sources, including the Departments of Agriculture, Defense, Energy, Health and Human Services, Interior, Justice, Labor, State, Treasury, and USAID. USAID is often, although not exclusively, the lead for implementing U.S. programs in the region. The organization characterizes the programs it executes as intended to make the United States and the Western hemisphere "more peaceful, secure, and prosperous by strengthening the capacity of governments and private entities to combat crime, improve governance, address climate change, and create an economic environment in which the private sector can flourish and create jobs" (USAID, 2018d). Specifically, USAID notes that its targeted programs in Honduras have delivered "improvements in security, governance, and prosperity," while characterizing U.S. giving to Haiti as having contributed to "advances in long-term reconstruction and development, economic growth and job creation, health care and education services, and municipal governance" (USAID, 2018d). Additionally, since the region is prone to earthquakes, severe weather events, and other disasters, USAID's Office of Foreign Disaster Assistance, the lead agency for coordinating U.S. responses to disasters overseas, plays an important role in helping prepare regional partners to be more resilient and assists them in the event that disaster strikes (USAID, 2017c).

USAID has been present in Haiti for about 50 years. It describes its Haiti work as focused on building "a stable and economically viable Haiti," with specific attention to "long-term reconstruction and development, promoting economic growth, job creation and agricultural development, providing basic health care and education services, and improving the effectiveness of government" (USAID, 2018c, 2017a). Foreign assistance from the United States, Taiwan, and other nations was particularly critical in the wake of the massive 2010 earthquake that killed approximately 230,000 people, and again in the aftermath of the Category 5 Hurricane Matthew in late 2016 that claimed at least 842 people and leveled large swathes of the country's already-fragile infrastructure (Ahmed, 2016). Even less powerful storms, such as the Hurricanes

Fay, Gustav, Hanna, and Ike in 2008, have "decimated Haiti's agricultural production, flooded towns, killed close to 800 people, and destroyed or damaged nearly 100,000 homes" (Baptiste, 2017). Recognizing Haiti's extreme vulnerability to natural disasters, USAID's Office of Foreign Disaster Assistance maintains a continuous presence in Haiti "in order to focus on providing immediate humanitarian assistance to disaster-affected populations and supporting disaster risk reduction programs" (USAID, 2017a).

In Honduras, USAID has carried out more than US$3 billion of economic assistance programs since 1961 (USAID, 2017c). These programs have been designed to

> strengthen the participation of marginalized groups in local and national governance; increase food security for the poorest sectors of society; support renewable energy and environmental conservation; expand basic education and skills training for at-risk youth and adults; and enhance citizen access to quality public education and health services by improving the performance of local governments, authorities, and civil society. (USAID, 2017b)

U.S. assistance programs are also designed to "address citizen security through community-based crime prevention activities" and seek to "spur economic growth, advance social justice, improve education and health, engage the poorest members of Honduran society in the country's development, and support public-private efforts to halt corruption and improve transparency" (USAID, 2018b). While USAID's efforts in Honduras focus mostly on economic development, good governance, and social programs, as one interviewee for this project noted, 1998's Category 5 Hurricane Mitch showed that disaster preparedness and resilience will remain a critical aspect of USAID's work for years to come since, without it, "decades of development can be wiped out in just a few days" (RAND interview #1).

Indeed, reflecting the region's vulnerability to natural disasters, Haiti has consistently been in the top three countries receiving the most U.S. assistance in the Western hemisphere since 2008 and has frequently been the number one U.S. aid recipient in the region in the past decade. Over the same period, Honduras has ranked as low as number 11 and as high as number four in terms of destination countries for U.S. aid (see Table 3.1).

The next section provides insights into U.S. officials' views of Taiwan's role in the LAC region.

## U.S. Views of Taiwan's Aid to Latin America and the Caribbean

The Three Communiqués between the United States and China (the Shanghai Communiqué, the Joint Communiqué, and the August 17th Communiqué), the Taiwan Relations Act, and the Six Assurances to Taiwan form the core of U.S.-China policy and govern policy toward Taiwan. U.S. officials, however, have frequently expressed their appreciation of the shared values of the United States and Taiwan and have praised Taiwan's constructive role in international society (Kelly, 2004; Kan and Morrison, 2014). While Erikson and Chen could ask, in 2007, if Washington cares about China's efforts to peel off Taiwan's diplomatic recognition in the LAC region, in 2019, U.S. policy goals for Taiwan in the Western hemisphere clearly identify helping Taiwan preserve its status and living space, while also working with the ROC closely

**Table 3.1**
**Dollar Value of U.S. Assistance to Haiti and Honduras, 2008–2018**

| Year | Haiti | Ranking | Honduras | Ranking |
|------|-------|---------|----------|---------|
| 2008 | $288 | 2 out of 36 | $72 | 8 out of 36 |
| 2009 | $389 | 3 out of 36 | $44 | 11 out of 36 |
| 2010 | $1,366 | 1 out of 35 | $40 | 11 out of 35 |
| 2011 | $586 | 1 out of 35 | $93 | 6 out of 35 |
| 2012 | $477 | 2 out of 35 | $69 | 7 out of 35 |
| 2013 | $365 | 2 out of 36 | $102 | 6 out of 36 |
| 2014 | $355 | 2 out of 33 | $96 | 6 out of 33 |
| 2015 | $502 | 3 out of 35 | $134 | 7 out of 35 |
| 2016 | $377 | 1 out of 34 | $128 | 4 out of 34 |
| 2017 | $307 | 2 out of 34 | $181 | 5 out of 34 |
| 2018[a] | $116 | 2 out of 32 | $31 | 5 out of 32 |

NOTES: All numbers rounded to nearest million.
[a] Data from 2008–2018 (USAID, undated[b]). As of late May 2018, data for 2017 and 2018 had only been partially reported; as of late January 2019, data for 2018 had only been partially reported (USAID, undated[a]).

to promote desirable regional outcomes, as priorities (Erikson and Chen, 2007, p. 82). As one interviewee for this study explained,

> U.S. interests in Latin America and the Caribbean include helping preserve Taiwan's access to the international community and ensuring that it is not cut-off entirely. To this end, the U.S. government now coordinates across departments and agencies to ensure that all relevant parts of the bureaucracy focused on the Western Hemisphere are attentive to this interest. (RAND interview #6A)

Reflecting this interest in areas outside the Department of State's Bureau of East Asian and Pacific Affairs, in March 2016, then–Principle Deputy Assistant Secretary for Economic and Business Affairs Kurt Tong stated that Taiwan's "evolution into a robust democracy, and a strong free market economy, with a vibrant civil society, make it a model for other [nations to follow]" and that Taiwan was a "responsible global citizen" that, through its partnership with PADF, had helped provide critical "training for disaster resilience and emergency preparedness" in the LAC region (Tong, 2016). James Moriarty, chair of AIT, offered a similar assessment, stating that the U.S. commitment to supporting Taiwan's role in international society has "never been stronger," describing Taiwan as "a force for good in the world [that] merits our continued strong support" (Moriarty, 2018). And AIT director Brent Christensen, in his first public remarks after assuming his position in fall 2018, commented on the "remarkable history" of U.S-Taiwan relations, noting Taiwan's development into "both a hi-tech economic powerhouse and also a highly successfully liberal democracy" with which the United States shares "so many values, including respect for the rule of law and support for civil liberties . . . [and] common interests," giving the two sides both a "strong foundation [and] a bright future" (Christensen, 2018). Such statements tend to reflect a warmth and normative or emotive dimension not characteristic of simple formal characterizations of relations with another country.

U.S. interviewees for this study repeatedly described Taiwan's approach to development assistance as praiseworthy and contrasted it sharply with China's regional aid programs. As one interlocutor stated, "If you work with Taiwan, you get an intimate partner that listens to your needs and cares about your feedback, whereas if you choose to opt for China, you get substantially less attention to your country's needs" (RAND interview #6A). As another interviewee commented, Taiwan "does development assistance the right way. By contrast, China is extractive, exploitive, and has a tendency to engage in checkbook diplomacy" that is divorced from the kinds of long-term partnerships with local communities that produce equitable, sustainable development (RAND interview #4). A third commentator pointed out that "cultural sensitivity to local conditions is a major asset that Taiwan brings to the table that China does not" (RAND interview #6B). A fourth expert, with over 15 years in the LAC region, noted that China "doesn't do much work in terms of capacity-building; they primarily just donate money during emergencies. It's not clear that they care whether or not this actually trickles down from the top to support local disaster relief and recovery efforts" (RAND interview #1). These views echo the conclusions of recent scholarly comparisons of the aid and assistance programs, modalities, and focus areas of Taiwan and China, with Taipei focusing on technical cooperation (often described as a "people-oriented approach" focused on "software" and skills training) and Beijing emphasizing infrastructural investment ("hardware") (see, for example, Lin and Lin, 2017).

Reflecting U.S. interest in finding creative ways to work with Taiwan in the absence of official diplomatic ties, the United States has in recent years cooperated with Taiwan to launch the Global Cooperation and Training Framework (GCTF). At its launch on June 1, 2015, AIT director Christopher Marut noted that the United States and Taiwan had already cooperated to deliver substantial assistance to countries facing health emergencies in Africa and the Middle East, while also coordinating closely on economic development in the Asia-Pacific, stating that the GCTF would "build upon these successes and explore new ways to harness U.S. and Taiwan capabilities and expertise for the benefit of regional and global communities" ("Taiwan, U.S. Sign MOU to Extend Partnership in Global Health, Aid," 2015). Speaking at the same GCTF launch event, then–Assistant Secretary of State for Economic and Business Affairs Charles Rivkin described the United States and Taiwan as "two like-minded partners working to create new opportunities to demonstrate the meaning of global citizenship" (Rivkin, 2015). The GCTF program brings developing country officials, civil society activists, scholars, and NGO workers to Taiwan for a series of meetings, where they can benefit from Taiwan's experience with development, disaster preparedness, and disaster recovery. It is also an opportunity for key figures from around the world to experience what life in the ROC is like firsthand over the course of the program of activities, building both their knowledge of Taiwan and their networks with Taiwan-based officials, experts, and activists. By situating the training programs in a U.S.-Taiwan context (AIT personnel and other Americans jointly participate), the United States makes clear that it cares about and values Taiwan's autonomy and participation in international society. To date, the GCTF has held seminars on energy efficiency; promoting e-commerce; laboratory diagnosis of dengue fever and the Zika virus and combatting mosquito-borne illnesses; women's empowerment; disaster relief; and closing the digital divide (AIT, undated[a]).

U.S. interviewees for this study repeatedly mentioned the GCTF as an important avenue for deepening U.S.-Taiwan cooperation and delivering meaningful and valued outcomes to the LAC region. The United States would "like to expand the focus of the GCTF to include Latin

America and the Caribbean in the future," one interviewee noted, pointing out that while, to date, all GCTF events have taken place in Taiwan, it could be useful to consider holding the next session in the LAC region (RAND interview #4). Another U.S. interviewee expressed hope that Taiwan can continue to devote "sufficient resources" as well as "top leadership attention" to its aid and development programs in the LAC region, believing that this would be crucial for slowing the erosion of the ROC's diplomatic presence in the region (RAND interview #6B).[1]

Another option that came up frequently in discussions with U.S. interlocutors was the value of Taiwan working through international and multilateral organizations such as the Organization for American States (OAS) or development institutions such as PADF. As Timothy Rich and Andi Dahmer have noted, "Taiwan's ability to embed itself in the political and economic institutions of Central America may explain in part its success in the region compared to individual attempts to procure and maintain partnerships elsewhere" (Rich and Dahmer, 2017). One interviewee noted that Taiwan's aid directed through PADF may help strengthen Taipei's ties with the OAS (RAND interview #3); another noted that by working with PADF, Taiwan can more easily engage with both the OAS and the U.S. Department of State (RAND interview #2). Similarly, in their study of Taipei's diplomatic contest with Beijing, Daniel Erikson and Janice Chen conclude that working through multilateral channels such as the OAS and the Inter-American Development Bank, together with free trade agreements and a smart approach to leveraging civil society NGOs, is a strategy for bolstering the ROC's aid that plays to Taiwan's strengths and comparative advantages (though they ultimately conclude that Taiwan's experience has shown that "nothing is quite as effective at making and keeping friends as straight cash payments funneled surreptitiously into private accounts") (Erikson and Chen, 2007, pp. 76–77).

Like Taiwan, USAID works closely with PADF in the LAC region and has done so for decades, including in Honduras and Haiti (PADF, undated[a]). Such shared interests in promoting common outcomes, including development, resilience, relief and the preservation of Taiwan's meaningful participation in international society suggest that cooperation between Taiwan and U.S. assistance programs will continue to be seen favorably for years to come.

## Conclusion

U.S. policy seeks similar outcomes to those promoted by the ROC's assistance programs in the LAC region generally and with respect to Haiti and Honduras specifically. Additionally, U.S. officials favorably regard, and U.S. policy supports, the continuation of Taiwan's diplomatic partnerships with countries in the LAC region. The United States seeks to promote this goal by cooperating on development and disaster relief with Taiwan through the GCTF and other avenues, as well as via direct indications of dissatisfaction with regional states if they break ties with Taipei. The final chapter describes the overall findings of the report and offers suggestions

---

[1]   As the loss of numerous diplomatic partners over the past three decades has shown, however, that such an approach alone is unlikely to arrest the erosion in the ROC's status. As noted earlier, for reasons related to both budget and focus, this study could not examine what the dimensions of a full, proactive strategy for arresting Taiwan's loss of diplomatic partners would look like nor does it assess its likely prospects of success. However, maintaining aid and senior-level attention appears to be an essential prerequisite.

for next steps that Taiwan can focus on as it seeks to defend its diplomatic standing in the LAC region through its overseas assistance programs.

# CHAPTER FOUR

# Conclusion: Optimizing Taiwan's Aid and Assistance to Latin America and the Caribbean

Taiwan's aid and assistance to Latin America and the Caribbean make important contributions to regional development, disaster resilience, and recovery, as well as to Taiwan's ability to hold onto diplomatic recognition from its ten remaining partner states based in the LAC region. At the same time, Taipei's assistance programs are just one factor among many in regional states' diplomatic alignment decisions. Shared history and common values, trade, and investment relations also matter, as do perceptions about U.S. reactions to any prospective decision to switch recognition from the ROC to the PRC and the contributions of Taiwan's vibrant civil society and private sector to regional development, which also shape partner nations' decisions about diplomatic recognition. Importantly, as noted at the outset of this report, since Taipei cannot match Beijing dollar for dollar, it must spend smartly and leverage its comparative strengths, including its reputation as a development miracle and a country that survives in a particularly difficult environment characterized by natural threats similar to those confronted by nations in the LAC region as well as one that promotes development and values favored by partner nations. This is not to suggest, however, that aid and assistance are not critical; they are clearly strong and valuable tools for preserving the diplomatic recognition that countries in the LAC region extend to the ROC. For this reason, the first conclusion of this study is that continued substantial funding and high-level leadership attention from Taiwan is critical to the effective employment of aid and assistance as a tool in Taipei's foreign policy kit.

Still, Taiwan's aid programs are a necessary but not sufficient tool for retaining diplomatic recognition, and Taiwan must be careful to protect its image against the perception—deserved or not—that it is merely "buying" (or worse, "renting") friendship from its diplomatic partners. Taiwan's approach to aid and development assistance is premised on working with and empowering local communities, a development strategy that is starkly different from China's infrastructure-centric assistance programs. Moreover, the interpersonal relationships that Taiwan officials, philanthropic civil society actors, and students cultivate when they go abroad are an important way of situating Taiwan's aid as part of a broader relationship and embedding it in a long-term partnership that is contingent on, and contributes to, preserving the ROC's diplomatic recognition.[1] As such, a second conclusion is that it is important for Taiwan to emphasize repeatedly that it offers assistance as a partnership with recipient countries, not a top-down transfer of infrastructure. Such an approach will be critical in helping partner

---

[1]  Erikson and Chen highlight the effective cultivation of elite networks in foreign partner nations as another important tactic for retaining diplomatic recognition (Erikson and Chen, 2007, pp. 73–74).

nations see that Taiwan is committed to their well-being over the long-run and that the ROC sees itself as a peer and a partner, not a distant great power using them for its own purposes.

The third conclusion is that the effectiveness of Taipei's aid and assistance programs would be bolstered by more explicitly building its programs into a framework that recognizes that they are merely one component of the broader relationships Taiwan has with its diplomatic partners in the region. The economic ties of trade and investment Taipei enjoys are a critical factor in supplementing its direct assistance programs. Additional research is warranted that would identify how important trade and investment are and where Taipei could increase its economic links to enhance the incentives that regional partners face to continue recognizing Taiwan. Recent work by Rich and Dahmer has suggested that China's expanding trading relationship with the region may explain countries' decisions to shift recognition, a finding that they argue means that Taipei should "no longer focus on international aid as a primary method in maintaining allies." Additionally, they argue, Taipei should "downplay the role of foreign aid in diplomatic relations and repackage efforts at maintaining diplomatic relations based on the need to stand up to Chinese efforts to isolate Taiwan internationally" to avoid creating incentives for diplomatic partners to attempt to extract greater concessions from Taipei (or alienating Taiwan voters and taxpayers who fear foreign partners may simply be trying to extract maximum resources from the ROC) (Rich and Dahmer, 2018). Instead, diplomatic recognition must be embedded in a broader, more meaningful, and more politically resilient bilateral relationship that includes Taiwan's investors and businesses.

A fourth and final conclusion from this research points to the recognition that Taiwan cannot be certain that under all circumstances will it be able to successfully hold onto its diplomatic partnerships in Latin America and the Caribbean. As one interviewee we spoke with argued, "telling Taiwan's story is not enough"[2]; another argued that there should be a high degree of urgency to craft a "positive approach—not just a fallback option or a strategy premised on making marginal adjustments but an effort to craft a bigger strategy" for repositioning Taiwan diplomatically in the world, something a third subject-matter expert argued would go well beyond "damage control" (RAND interviews #7B, #7D, and #7F, respectively). Such a larger strategy lies beyond the scope of this study. Still, in the interim, a less-ambitious strategy that smartly employs Taiwan's key financial, human capital, reputational, trade and investment, and informal diplomatic resources appears to hold some promise for preserving Taipei's international status and recognition in the region.

---

[2]  This interviewee meant that it is not enough to simply highlight Taiwan's democratic values and free-market capitalist economy to retain diplomatic ties; Taipei will need to be more active if it hopes to keep its few remaining sources of diplomatic recognition.

# References

Ahmed, Azam, "Hurricane Matthew Makes Old Problems Worse for Haitians," *New York Times*, October 6, 2016.

Alexander, Colin R., *China and Taiwan in* Central *America*, New York: Palgrave MacMillan, 2014.

AIT—*See* American Institute in Taiwan.

American Institute in Taiwan, "Global Cooperation and Training Framework (GCTF)," webpage, undated(a). As of February 1, 2019:
https://www.ait.org.tw/tag/gctf/

American Institute in Taiwan, "Our Relationship," webpage, undated(b). As of February 1, 2019:
https://www.ait.org.tw/our-relationship/

Baptiste, Nathalie, "Haiti Still Hasn't Recovered from Hurricane Matthew, Now Here Comes Irma," *Mother Jones*, September 7, 2017. As of February 1, 2019:
https://www.motherjones.com/environment/2017/09/
haiti-still-hasnt-recovered-from-hurricane-matthew-now-here-comes-irma/

Blanchard, Ben, "After Ditching Taiwan, China Says Panama Will Get the Help It Needs," Reuters, November 17, 2017.

Caldwell, Alicia A., "Trump Administration Ends Program for Honduran Immigrants," *Wall Street Journal*, May 4, 2018. As of February 1, 2019:
https://www.wsj.com/articles/trump-administration-ends-program-for-honduran-immigrants-1525465964

Campbell, Caitlin, and Zoe Valette, *China's Expanding and Evolving Engagement with the Caribbean*, Washington, D.C.: U.S.-China Economic and Security, May 16, 2014. As of February 1, 2019:
https://www.uscc.gov/sites/default/files/Research/Staff%20Report_China-Caribbean%20Relations.pdf

Christensen, Brent, "Remarks by AIT Director Brent Christensen at Press Conference," Washington, D.C.: American Institute in Taiwan, October 31, 2018. As of February 1, 2019:
https://www.ait.org.tw/remarks-by-ait-director-brent-christensen-at-press-conference/

Chung, Lawrence, "Dominican Republic Breaks with Taiwan, Forges Diplomatic Ties with Beijing," Associated Press, May 1, 2018.

Cole, J. Michael, "Panama Severs Diplomatic Relations with Taiwan," *Taiwan Sentinel*, June 13, 2017.

Council on Hemispheric Affairs, "The Big China and Taiwan Tussle: Dollar Diplomacy Returns to Latin America," webpage, September 19, 2008. As of January 31, 2019:
http://www.coha.org/the-big-china-and-taiwan-tussle-dollar-diplomacy-debuts-in-latin-america/

Davis, Julie Hirshfeld, Sheryl Gay Stolberg, and Thomas Kaplan, "Trump Alarms Lawmakers with Disparaging Words for Haiti and Africa," *New York Times*, January 11, 2018. As of February 1, 2019:
https://www.nytimes.com/2018/01/11/us/politics/trump-shithole-countries.html

Erikson, Daniel P., and Janice Chen, "China, Taiwan, and the Battle for Latin America," *The Fletcher Forum of World Affairs*, Vol. 31, No. 2, Summer 2007, pp. 69–89.

Fagen, Patricia Weiss, "Natural Disasters in Latin America and the Caribbean: National, Regional and International Interactions: A Regional Case Study on the Role of the Affected State in Humanitarian Action," Humanitarian Policy Group Working Paper, London: Humanitarian Policy Group, October 2008.

Gardner, Cory, "Gardner, Markey Introduce Legislation to Ensure Taiwan's Role on World Stage Is Not Diminished by China," Washington, D.C., May 25, 2018. As of February 1, 2019:
https://www.gardner.senate.gov/newsroom/press-releases/
gardner-markey-introduce-legislation-to-ensure-taiwans-role-on-world-stage-is-not-diminished-by-china

Her, Kelly, "Delivering Effective Aid," *Taiwan Today*, December 1, 2012. As of February 1, 2019:
https://taiwantoday.tw/news.php?unit=4,29,29,31,45&post=7953

Horton, Chris, "In Taiwan, U.S. Official Says Commitment 'Has Never Been Stronger,'" *New York Times*, March 21, 2018a. As of February 1, 2019:
https://www.nytimes.com/2018/03/21/world/asia/taiwan-china-alex-wong.html

Horton, Chris, "El Salvador Recognizes China in Blow to Taiwan," *New York Times*, August 21, 2018b.

ICDF—*See* Taiwan International Cooperation and Development Fund.

Inter-American Development Bank, "News Release: Latin America and Caribbean Exports to China Increased 30 Percent in 2017," webpage, December 18, 2017. As of February 1, 2019:
https://www.iadb.org/en/news/news-releases/2017-12-18/trade-trend-estimates-2018%2C12017.html

Jones, Sam, "World Heading for Catastrophe over Natural Disasters, Risk Expert Warns," *The Guardian*, April 24, 2016. As of January 31, 2019:
https://www.theguardian.com/global-development/2016/apr/24/
world-heading-for-catastrophe-over-natural-disasters-risk-expert-warns

Kan, Shirley A., and Wayne M. Morrison, *U.S.-Taiwan Relationship: Overview of Policy Issues*, Washington, D.C.: Congressional Research Service, R41952, December 11, 2014. As of February 1, 2019:
https://fas.org/sgp/crs/row/R41952.pdf

Kang, Inyoung, "A List of Previous Disasters in Haiti, a Land All Too Familiar with Hardship," *New York Times*, October 4, 2016. As of January 31, 2019:
https://www.nytimes.com/2016/10/05/world/americas/haiti-hurricane-earthquake.html

Kelly, James, "Overview of U.S. Policy Toward Taiwan," testimony at hearing on Taiwan, House International Relations Committee, Washington, D.C., April 21, 2004. As of February 1, 2019:
https://2001-2009.state.gov/p/eap/rls/rm/2004/31649.htm

Khan, Haider A., "Technology and Economic Development: The Case of Taiwan," *Journal of Contemporary China*, Vol. 13, No. 40, 2004, pp. 507–521.

Koleski, Katherine, and Alec Blivas, *China's Engagement with Latin America and the Caribbean*, Washington, D.C.: U.S.-China Economic and Security Review Commission, October 17, 2018. As of February 1, 2019:
https://www.uscc.gov/sites/default/files/Research/China%27s%20Engagement%20with%20Latin%20
America%20and%20the%20Caribbean_.pdf

Lin, Teh-Chang, and Jean Yen-Chun Lin, "Taiwan's Foreign Aid in Transition: From ODA to Civil Society Approaches," *Japanese Journal of Political Science*, Vol. 18, No. 4, December 2017, pp. 469–490.

Lu, I-Hsuan, and Sherry Hsiao, "Taiwan Force for Good in World, U.S. Official Says," *Taipei Times*, April 28, 2018. As of February 1, 2019:
http://www.taipeitimes.com/News/taiwan/archives/2018/04/28/2003692139

Lu, Zhenhua, "U.S. Urges China–Taiwan 'Dialogue' Despite Panama's Jilting of Taipei," *South China Morning Post*, June 14, 2017. As of February 1, 2019
https://www.scmp.com/news/asia/diplomacy/article/2098212/
us-urges-china-taiwan-dialogue-despite-panamas-jilting-taipei

Maggiorelli, Lorenzo, "Chinese Aid to Latin America and the Caribbean: Evolution and Prospects," *Inicio*, Vol. 4, No. 2, 2017.

Malkin, Elisabeth, "Taiwan Works to Keep Its Central American Friends (Among Its Few)," *New York Times*, January 13, 2017.

Menchu, Sofia, "Taiwan's Central American Allies Coy on Panama's Beijing Embrace," Reuters, June 13, 2017.

Ministry of Foreign Affairs of the People's Republic of China, "China's Policy Paper on Latin America and the Caribbean," Beijing, November 24, 2016. As of February 1, 2019:
http://english.gov.cn/archive/white_paper/2016/11/24/content_281475499069158.htm

Ministry of Foreign Affairs, Republic of China (Taiwan), *International Cooperation and Development Report 2010*, January 3, 2012. As of February 1, 2019:
https://www.mofa.gov.tw/Upload/RelFile/17/262/fe7c546c-1159-4867-ae80-e5eec9f8b625.pdf

Ministry of Foreign Affairs, Republic of China (Taiwan), *International Cooperation and Development Report 2013*, April 29, 2014. As of February 1, 2019:
https://www.mofa.gov.tw/Upload/RelFile/17/262/cb6707b1-a9d4-49a1-a162-f42b71c50e68.pdf

Ministry of Foreign Affairs, Republic of China (Taiwan), *International Cooperation and Development Report 2014*, April 14, 2015. As of February 1, 2019:
https://www.mofa.gov.tw/Upload/RelFile/17/262/f7a8056d-26f6-4fdf-80be-c2963619f7de.pdf

Ministry of Foreign Affairs, Republic of China (Taiwan), "Foreign Policy Guidelines," webpage, June 1, 2016. As of February 1, 2019:
https://www.mofa.gov.tw/en/cp.aspx?n=B7411BDCD003C9EC

Ministry of Foreign Affairs, Republic of China (Taiwan), "Diplomatic Allies," webpage, January 29, 2019. As of January 31, 2019:
https://www.mofa.gov.tw/en/AlliesIndex.aspx?n=DF6F8F246049F8D6&sms=A76B7230ADF29736

Morgan, Daniela Estrella, "Trade Developments in Latin America and the Caribbean," Washington, D.C.: International Monetary Fund, March 2017.

Moriarty, James, "The United States and Taiwan: An Enduring Partnership, Remarks by AIT Chairman James Moriarty at Stanford University," Palo Alto, Calif.: Stanford University, May 3, 2018. As of February 1, 2019:
https://www.ait.org.tw/the-us-and-taiwan-an-enduring-partnership-remarks/

"Moy Reaffirms U.S.' Support for Taiwan at WHA," *Taipei Times*, April 24, 2018. As of February 1, 2019:
http://www.taipeitimes.com/News/front/archives/2018/04/24/2003691885

Myers, Margaret, and Kevin Gallagher, *Down but Not Out: Chinese Development Finance in LAC, 2017*, Washington, D.C.: The Dialogue, March 2018. As of February 1, 2019:
https://www.thedialogue.org/wp-content/uploads/2018/03/Chinese-Finance-to-LAC-2017-Updated.pdf

Ndiaga, Thiam, and Jess Macy Yu, "Taiwan 'Sad, Angry' as It Loses Second Ally in a Month Amid China Pressure," Reuters, May 24, 2018.

Nicholson, George, "Transport, Logistics and Competitiveness in the Caribbean," *Caribbean Journal*, September 2015. As of January 31, 2019:
https://www.caribjournal.com/2015/09/04/transport-logistics-and-competitiveness-in-the-caribbean/

PADF—*See* Pan American Development Foundation.

Pan American Development Foundation, "History of PADF," webpage, undated(a). As of February 1, 2019:
https://www.padf.org/history/

Pan American Development Foundation, "Our Mission," webpage, undated(b). As of February 1, 2019:
https://www.padf.org/our-mission/

Pan American Development Foundation, "Public Partners," webpage, undated(c). As of February 1, 2019:
https://www.padf.org/public-partners

Pan American Development Foundation, *Disaster Preparedness and Mitigation Project in the Southeast Department of Haiti and the Border Region of the Dominican Republic, Final Report, April–October 2013*, Washington, D.C., December 6, 2013a.

Pan American Development Foundation, *A Neighborhood-Based Approach to Disaster Risk Reduction for Highly Vulnerable Hillside Communities in Tegucigalpa, Honduras*, Final Report, Washington, D.C., December 17, 2013b.

Pan American Development Foundation, *Taiwan and PADF Disaster Assistance and Reconstruction Fund for Latin America and the Caribbean: 2015 Annual Report*, Washington, D.C., January 29, 2016.

Pence, Mike, "Vice President Mike Pence's Remarks on the Administration's Policy Towards China October 4 Event," Washington, D.C.: Hudson Institute, October 4, 2018. As of February 1, 2019:
https://www.hudson.org/events/1610-vice-president-mike-pence-s-remarks-on-the-administration-s-policy-towards-china102018

Pompeo, Michael R., "Remarks on 'America's Indo-Pacific Economic Vision,'" Washington, D.C.: U.S. Chamber of Commerce, Indo-Pacific Business Forum, July 30, 2018. As of February 1, 2019:
https://www.state.gov/secretary/remarks/2018/07/284722.htm

Ramos, Adele, "Taiwan Gives Guatemala over US$600 Million in Funding," *Amandala* (Belize), August 9, 2017.

Reuters, "Panama Breaks with Taiwan as It Establishes Ties with China," June 12, 2017.

Reuters, "U.S. Recalls Diplomats in El Salvador, Panama, Dominican Republic over Taiwan," September 7, 2018.

Rich, Timothy, "Haitian Disaster Relief: Implications of Chinese and Taiwanese Assistance," *The Newsletter*, No. 53, Spring 2010. As of February 1, 2019:
https://iias.asia/sites/default/files/IIAS_NL53_09.pdf

Rich, Timothy, and Andi Dahmer, "Taiwan's Central America Dilemma," *Taiwan Sentinel*, September 21, 2017. As of February 1, 2019:
https://sentinel.tw/taiwans-central-america-dilemma/

Rich, Timothy, and Andi Dahmer, "Taiwan, International Aid, and the Challenge of Official Recognition," *Taiwan Sentinel*, May 6, 2018. As of February 1, 2019:
https://sentinel.tw/taiwan-intl-aid-recognition/

Rivkin, Charles H., "Remarks by Assistant Secretary of State Charles H. Rivkin at Global Cooperation Training Framework (GCTF) MOU Signing Ceremony," Taipei, Taiwan: American Institute in Taiwan, June 1, 2015. As of February 1, 2019:
https://www.ait.org.tw/remarks-assistant-secretary-state-charles-h-rivkin-global-cooperation-training-framework-gctf-mou-signing-ceremony/

Southerland, Dan, "China Makes Inroads in Caribbean Nations Through Aid, Trade," *Radio Free Asia*, August 30, 2017. As of February 1, 2019:
https://www.rfa.org/english/commentaries/caribbean-china-08302017165130.html

"Statement from the Press Secretary on El Salvador," White House, August 23, 2018. As of February 1, 2019:
https://www.whitehouse.gov/briefings-statements/statement-press-secretary-el-salvador/

Sullivan, Mark P., and Thomas Lum, "In Focus: China's Engagement with Latin America and the Caribbean," Washington, D.C.: Congressional Research Service, 7-5700, September 18, 2018. As of February 1, 2019:
https://fas.org/sgp/crs/row/IF10982.pdf

Taiwan International Cooperation and Development Fund, "About Us," webpage, undated(a). As of February 1, 2019:
http://www.icdf.org.tw/ct.asp?xItem=4470&CtNode=29840&mp=2

Taiwan International Cooperation and Development Fund, "About Us > Executive Officers," webpage, undated(b). As of January 31, 2019:
http://www.icdf.org.tw/ct.asp?xItem=5196&ctNode=29841&mp=2

Taiwan International Cooperation and Development Fund, "About Us > Status," webpage, undated(c). As of February 1, 2019:
https://www.icdf.org.tw/ct.asp?xItem=4583&CtNode=29845&mp=2

Taiwan International Cooperation and Development Fund, "Bilateral Projects, Central America and South America," webpage, undated(d). As of May 15, 2018:
https://www.icdf.org.tw/np.asp?ctNode=29986&mp=2.

Taiwan International Cooperation and Development Fund, "Caribbean," webpage, undated(e). As of February 1, 2019: https://www.icdf.org.tw/lp.asp?ctNode=29867&CtUnit=199&BaseDSD=101&mp=2

Taiwan International Cooperation and Development Fund, "Guatemala," webpage, undated(f). As of January 31, 2019:
https://www.icdf.org.tw/lp.asp?ctNode=30062&CtUnit=172&BaseDSD=100&mp=2

Taiwan International Cooperation and Development Fund, "History > History of the Taiwan ICDF," webpage, December 6, 2010. As of February 1, 2019:
http://www.icdf.org.tw/ct.asp?xItem=4582&ctNode=29843&mp=2

Taiwan International Cooperation and Development Fund, "Embracing the Earth, Preserving Our Planet: New Hope Village Water Supply System Project," YouTube.com, April 20, 2014. As of January 30, 2019:
https://www.youtube.com/watch?v=iyvmQ-DFQ7k

"Taiwan, U.S. Sign MOU to Extend Partnership in Global Health, Aid," *Focus Taiwan*, June 1, 2015. As of February 1, 2019:
http://focustaiwan.tw/news/aipl/201506010011.aspx

Tannenbaum, Ben, "Filling the Void: China's Expanding Caribbean Presence," Council on Hemispheric Affairs, April 3, 2018. As of February 1, 2019:
http://www.coha.org/filling-the-void-chinas-expanding-caribbean-presence/

Tong, Kurt, "Taiwan's International Role and the GCTF," Washington, D.C., March 2, 2016. As of February 1, 2019:
https://2009-2017.state.gov/e/eb/rls/rm/2016/253915.htm

Tubilewicz, Czeslaw, and Alain Guilloux, "Does Size Matter? Foreign Aid in Taiwan's Diplomatic Strategy, 2000–2008," *Australian Journal of International Affairs*, Vol. 65, No. 3, June 2011, pp. 322–339.

United Nations, "Towards a New Aid Architecture," Chapter III in *World Economic and Social Survey 2010*, New York, 2010, pp. 47–70.

U.S. Agency for International Development, "Explorer," webpage, undated(a). As of February 1, 2019:
https://explorer.usaid.gov/

U.S. Agency for International Development, "Foreign Aid Explorer: U.S. Foreign Aid by Country," webpage, undated(b). As of February 1, 2019:
https://explorer.usaid.gov/cd

U.S. Agency for International Development, "Haiti—Country Profile," flier, March 2017a.

U.S. Agency for International Development, "Office of U.S. Foreign Disaster Assistance," webpage, July 18, 2017b. As of February 1, 2019:
https://www.usaid.gov/who-we-are/organization/bureaus/
bureau-democracy-conflict-and-humanitarian-assistance/office-us

U.S. Agency for International Development, "Honduras: History," webpage, November 20, 2017c. As of February 1, 2019:
https://www.usaid.gov/honduras/history

U.S. Agency for International Development, "Missions, Visions and Values," webpage, February 18, 2018a. As of February 1, 2019:
https://www.usaid.gov/who-we-are/mission-vision-values

U.S. Agency for International Development, "Honduras," webpage, July 18, 2018b. As of February 1, 2019:
https://www.usaid.gov/honduras

U.S. Agency for International Development, "Haiti: History," webpage, August 16, 2018c. As of February 1, 2019:
https://www.usaid.gov/haiti/history

U.S. Agency for International Development, "Latin America and the Caribbean," webpage, November 19, 2018d. As of February 1, 2019:
https://www.usaid.gov/where-we-work/latin-american-and-caribbean

USAID—*See* U.S. Agency for International Development.

U.S. Department of State, "Bureau of Western Hemisphere Affairs," webpage, undated. As of February 1, 2019:
https://www.state.gov/p/wha/index.htm

U.S. Department of State, Bureau of East Asian and Pacific Affairs, "U.S. Relations with Taiwan," webpage, August 31, 2018. As of February 1, 2019:
https://www.state.gov/r/pa/ei/bgn/35855.htm

"U.S. Lawmakers Introduce TAIPEI Act," *Taipei Times*, September 7, 2018. As of February 1, 2019:
http://www.taipeitimes.com/News/front/archives/2018/09/07/2003699941

"U.S. Says It Is Disappointed with Burkina Faso Switch," *Taipei Times*, May 27, 2018. As of February 1, 2019:
http://www.taipeitimes.com/News/taiwan/archives/2018/05/27/2003693810

Yu, Jess Macy, and Ben Blanchard, "Taiwan Says China Dangled $3 Billion to Grab Ally Dominican Republic," Reuters, April 30, 2018.